The Merchant of Venice

A Shakespeare Story

RETOLD BY ANDREW MATTHEWS
ILLUSTRATED BY TONY ROSS

ORCHARD

For May, with love
A.M.

ORCHARD BOOKS
338 Euston Road, London NW1 3BH
Orchard Books Australia
Hachette Children's Books
Level 17/207 Kent St, Sydney, NSW 2000
First published in Great Britain in 2009
First paperback publication in 2010
This slipcase edition published in 2013
Not for individual resale
Text © Andrew Matthews 2009
Illustrations © Tony Ross 2009
ISBN 978 1 40780 976 2
The rights of Andrew Matthews to be identified as the author and Tony Ross as
the illustrator of this work have been asserted by them in accordance with the
Copyright, Designs and Patents Act, 1988.
A CIP catalogue record for this book is available from the British Library
Printed in China

Orchard Books is a division of Hachette Childrens Books,
an Hachette UK company.
www.hachette.co.uk

Contents

Cast List

Antonio

A Venetian merchant

Bassanio

Antonio's young friend,
in love with Portia

Portia

A noblewoman of Belmont,
in love with Bassanio

Nerissa

Portia's maid

Shylock
A Venetian moneylender

The Prince of Arragon
Portia's suitor

The Prince of Morocco
Portia's suitor

The Duke of Venice
Judge at Antonio's trial

The Scene
Venice in the sixteenth century.

I will buy with you, sell with you,
walk with you and so following;
but I will not eat with you, drink with you,
nor pray with you.

Shylock; I.iii.

The Merchant of Venice

One afternoon in the city of Venice, two
men stood together on a bridge over
a canal. The older man, Antonio, was a
successful merchant. His companion was

his friend Bassanio. Antonio had just told Bassanio a scandalous piece of gossip, but Bassanio did not seem interested.

"What's wrong, Bassanio?" said Antonio. "You've hardly spoken a word to me."

Bassanio peered down at the canal. "Last year, I visited the town of Belmont. I had dinner there with a man who had a beautiful daughter, named Portia," he said.

She was wise, witty—"

"And you fell in love with her?" interrupted Antonio.

Bassanio blushed. "I've been thinking about her ever since," he confessed. "Two days ago, I learned that Portia's father has died, leaving her all his fortune. She is one of the richest women in Italy."

Antonio slapped his friend on the back. "Then go to Belmont, and woo her!" he urged.

"Rich suitors are flocking to propose to Portia – even princes from foreign lands!" groaned Bassanio. "What chance would I stand against them? I can't even afford a new suit of clothes!"

"How much money do you need to woo Portia in style?" Antonio asked.

"Three thousand ducats," replied Bassanio.

Antonio lowered his voice, so that passers-by would not hear him. "If I had the money, I would lend it to you," he said. "But at the moment, I haven't got three hundred ducats, let alone three thousand. All my money is invested in four ships that are voyaging around the world. When they return to Venice, I'll be a wealthy man again, but until then..."

"So you can't help me?" Bassanio cried in despair.

"My reputation is still good," said Antonio. "Find a moneylender who will loan you three thousand ducats, and I will sign a bond promising to repay him."

Bassanio beamed. "You are the best friend a man could have!" he declared.

✳ ✳ ✳

While Bassanio and Antonio were talking on the bridge in Venice, in Belmont the lovely Portia paced to and fro across a richly furnished room. Her serving maid, Nerissa, watched from a chair in the corner. In the centre of the room was an oak table, and on it were three caskets – one made of gold, another of silver, and the third made of lead.

Suddenly, Portia stopped pacing, and stamped her foot. "This is so unfair!" she grumbled. "I'm an intelligent, educated woman, but can I choose a husband for myself? Oh no! The man who marries me must select one of these stupid caskets. If he picks the right one, I have to be his wife."

"That was one of the conditions of your father's will, Miss," said Nerissa. "If you hadn't agreed to it, you wouldn't have inherited his money." A far-off look came into Nerissa's eyes. "I know who I'd pick as a husband for you," she said.

"Who?" demanded Portia.

"That Venetian gentleman who came to dinner last summer," Nerissa cooed.

A faint redness crept into Portia's cheeks. "His name was Bassanio, wasn't it?" she said.

"So it was!" exclaimed Nerissa. "There was something special about him, and if you ask me, he thought you were special too, Miss."

Portia's cheeks turned a deeper red. "Nonsense!" she said. "Bassanio has probably forgotten all about me!"

* * *

As the sun set over Venice, Bassanio strolled around a public square, discussing business with Shylock the moneylender, who was a thin man with a long grizzled beard.

Shylock had a sharp mind, but often pretended to be slow-witted, to mislead his clients. He frowned at Bassanio, and said, "Let me be clear about this. You want to borrow three thousand ducats?"

"I do," said Bassanio.

"And your friend, the merchant Antonio, will sign a bond guaranteeing that he will pay back the money within three months?"

Bassanio nodded. "He will," he said. "Look, here comes Antonio now. He'll tell you himself."

Shylock narrowed his eyes. He and Antonio detested each other, though both

men made a show of being polite.

"Well, Shylock!" said Antonio. "Will you lend Bassanio the money?"

"I am considering it," Shylock replied. "It surprises me that you're willing to sign a bond. Didn't I hear you boast that you would never charge interest on a loan, or pay interest on any money that you borrowed?"

"Normally, I wouldn't," agreed Antonio. "But this money is for my friend, so I'm making an exception. Will you give him the money, or not?"

Shylock spoke quietly, but sparks of rage glowed in his eyes. "Antonio, you have often criticised the way I do business, but I have never complained," he said. "The other day, you spat on my clothes, called me a Jewish dog and kicked me. Today, you're asking for my help.

Remember that Jews are just as human as you. If you cut us, we bleed, if you poison us, we die – and if you insult us, we will have our revenge."

"We don't like each other, Shylock," Antonio said frankly. "If I don't return your loan in time, imagine the pleasure it will give you to make me pay the penalty."

Shylock laughed, as if he had thought of a joke. "Speaking of the penalty, I think it would be amusing if the lawyer who draws up the bond writes that if you do not pay me by such-and-such a date, you will let me cut off a pound of your flesh, from the place nearest your heart. Agree to that, and your friend shall have his money," he said.

Bassanio clutched Antonio's arm. "No, Antonio!" he gasped. "Let's find another moneylender."

Antonio sensed that Shylock was testing him. If he refused Shylock's terms, the moneylender would spread the word that Antonio was a coward.

"Just as you wish, Shylock," Antonio said.

"No!" said Bassanio. "What if something happens to your ships?"

"Don't worry!" Antonio said. "They are due back in Venice a month before the repayment date."

Neither Antonio nor Bassanio noticed Shylock's gloating smile.

Sailors make mistakes, and ships sink, Antonio! Shylock thought. *Once that bond is signed, you will be at my mercy!*

* * *

In Belmont, Portia led the Prince of Morocco into the room where the caskets were kept. The Prince was a handsome man, whose white robes showed off his dark skin. He stared at the caskets, picked up the one made of lead, and read the words inscribed on it. *"If you choose me, you must risk all that you have."*

The Prince put down the casket. "Risk all that I have – for lead?" he snorted. "I will risk nothing for a common metal.

What is the inscription on the silver casket? *If you choose me, you will get as much as you deserve.*" The Prince laughed. "This could be the right casket. I deserve the best, and Lady Portia would be the best wife for me.

But I'll wait until I've read the inscription on the gold casket. *If you choose me, you will get what many men desire.* This must be the one! Many men want to marry Lady Portia, and a prize like her must be in a casket made from the most precious metal of all!"

The Prince lifted the lid of the gold casket, and cried out in dismay. Inside was a human skull, with a small roll of parchment in one of its eye sockets.

The Prince unrolled the parchment,
and read:

All that glistens is not gold,
As you often have been told.
You have chosen outward show,
So now say farewell, and go.

Without another word, the Prince
left the room, and Portia heaved a sigh
of relief.

The next afternoon in Belmont, the
Prince of Arragon took his turn at
choosing between Portia's three caskets.
He stroked his beard, and spoke his
thoughts aloud. "Lead is too crude for my
taste," he said, "and gold is too obvious.
I choose the silver casket."

The Prince opened the casket, and found a miniature painting of a man dressed as a jester. With the painting was a parchment scroll, which read:

This picture makes it plain to see
That you have chosen foolishly.
Though you are strong, your mind is weak
And you are not the one I seek.

The Prince bowed to Portia. "I will not make an even bigger fool of myself by staying any longer, My Lady," he said, and left.

The next moment, Nerissa burst into the room. "You'll never guess who I met in town, Miss!" she jabbered. "Bassanio! He's on his way here to ask you to marry him. Isn't it romantic?"

Portia felt as excited as Nerissa, but kept her feelings hidden. "Romantic or not, he will have to take the test, like all the other suitors," she said solemnly.

✳ ✳ ✳

Bassanio and Portia were delighted to meet again. Portia explained the peculiar conditions of her father's will. Bassanio admitted that he was poor, and described how and why Antonio had borrowed money from Shylock.

Finally, Bassanio said, "Show me the caskets. Let me choose."

Portia was afraid. If Bassanio chose wrongly, she would lose him forever. "Wait a few days!" she begged.

"I can't bear to," said Bassanio. "I have to know if we're to spend our lives together, or apart."

Portia led Bassanio to the room where the caskets were kept, and he examined them. "Evil often disguises itself," he said. "In court, a guilty man hides his crime behind a clever argument. Cowardly soldiers mask their fear by pretending to be brave. But this lead casket doesn't seem to be hiding anything."

With shaking hands, Bassanio opened
the casket. Inside was a portrait of
Portia, and a scroll that read:

You have not chosen with your eyes,
But with your heart, and you are wise.
Turn now to where your lady is,
And claim her with a loving kiss.

So, Bassanio and Portia were married, and were blissfully happy. As the weeks turned into months, Bassanio almost forgot about his previous life. Then, one morning at breakfast, he received a letter from Venice. As he read the letter, he gasped in horror.

"Is it bad news?" enquired Portia.

"The worst!" Bassanio said. "Antonio's ships have been lost at sea. Shylock has had him thrown into prison, and says that Antonio must keep his bond."

"Give Shylock his three thousand ducats!" exclaimed Portia. "Give him six thousand if he wants."

"Shylock's daughter ran off and married a Christian. She took money from her father's cash boxes. The shock has hardened Shylock's heart," Bassanio said. "He insists on his pound of flesh. Antonio goes on trial for debt in a few days."

"We owe him our happiness," said Portia. "You must go and see him at once."

While Bassanio was packing for his trip, Portia called Nerissa to her, and told her about Antonio.

"Poor fellow!" Nerissa sighed.

"I'm going to help him!" announced Portia. "My cousin, Dr Bellario, taught me a lot about the law when I first tried to understand Father's will. I'll call on him, ask him for a letter of introduction to the Duke of Venice, and discuss Antonio's case. Then you and I are are off to Venice – disguised as lawyers!"

* * *

On the day of Antonio's trial, all Venice seemed to be packed into the courtroom. The Duke of Venice sat in the judge's chair, with Shylock to his left, and Antonio and Bassanio to his right.

The Duke signalled for silence, and said,

"Where is the lawyer Balthazar, sent by
Dr Bellario to defend Antonio?"

Portia and Nerissa stood up, and bowed.
They were wearing lawyers' robes, and
Portia had glued on a false beard. "Here
I am, My Lord!" she said in a deep voice.

"You may begin!" declared the Duke.

Portia turned to Shylock. "Will you give up the bond if Antonio returns the three thousand ducats he borrowed from you?" she asked.

"I would not give it up for sixty thousand ducats!" Shylock hissed.

"Antonio," Portia said, "were you tricked into signing the bond?"

"No," replied Antonio.

Portia shrugged. "Then the bond is legal, but Shylock must be merciful," she said.

"Merciful?" hooted Shylock. "Why must I be merciful?"

"Because mercy brings a blessing both to those who receive it, and those who give it," Portia told him.

"I don't want to be blessed!" grunted Shylock. "I want justice to be done!"

"Show me the bond!" said Portia.

The Clerk of the Court handed her a parchment, which she read quickly. "The moneylender is right," she said. "The law is on his side. Antonio, unfasten your shirt, and prepare to die."

"Give me your hand, Bassanio!" whispered Antonio. "Goodbye, my friend!"

Shylock produced a dagger, and began to sharpen it on a small stone.

"Take care when you cut, Shylock," Portia advised.

"Why?" snapped Shylock.

"According to the bond, you can cut off a pound of Antonio's flesh from the place closest to his heart, but there is no

mention of blood," Portia said. "Shed one drop of his blood, and the state of Venice will confiscate everything you own."

Shylock knew that he had been outwitted. He glowered at Portia.

"Give me my three thousand ducats!" he snarled.

"You have already refused the money in open court," Portia pointed out.

The Duke spoke severely to Shylock. "According to the laws of Venice," he said, "if someone plots to take another's life, half his property will be confiscated by the state, and the other half will be given to his intended victim."

Shylock's face went pale. "I have lost everything!" he whimpered. "You may as well sentence me to death!"

"Will you show Shylock any mercy, Antonio?" said Portia.

Antonio looked at Shylock, and saw not a loathed enemy, but a broken old man. "I wish to end the hatred between us," he said. "Let Shylock keep my half of his property, as long as he agrees to become a Christian."

The Duke stood up. "The case is closed," he said. "All are free to go."

The crowd in the courtroom cheered, and chanted Antonio's name.

Bassanio forced his way through the throng, and caught Portia by the arm. "Master Balthazar, you have saved my best friend's life!" he gushed. "I swear that I will give you anything you ask for."

Portia smiled.
"Then I will
have your gold
ring," she said.

Bassanio's
face fell. "That is
my wedding ring!"
he said. "I swore to my wife
that I would always keep it safe."

"And you swore to me
that you would give
me anything
I asked for," said
Portia. "Your
wife is married
to a man who
thinks nothing
of breaking
promises."

Reluctantly, Bassanio removed the ring, and presented it to Portia. "When she learns how much I owe you, my

wife will understand why I gave you my wedding ring."

"Oh, I know she will!" Portia assured him.

Then she and Nerissa slipped away, and left Venice to its celebrations.

The quality of mercy is not strain'd
It droppeth as the gentle rain from heaven
Upon the place beneath: it is twice blest;
It blesseth him that gives, and him that takes.

Portia; IV.i.

Love, Hate and Mercy in The Merchant of Venice

The story closest to the plot of *The Merchant of Venice* appeared in a collection of stories by the Italian writer, Ser Giovanni, which was published in Milan in 1558. Shakespeare probably used it as the basis of his play, which he wrote some time between 1596 and 1597. Though *The Merchant of Venice* comes very close to tragedy, it is classed as a comedy because of its happy ending.

Shylock is a villain, not because he is a Jew, but because greed and hatred have twisted his personality. He considers Antonio a fool for not charging interest on the money that he lends.

Antonio has good qualities – he is a loyal and generous friend – but his treatment of Shylock is shameful, and it is easy to understand why Shylock wants to be revenged on him. The merchant is also rash, or he would never have agreed to Shylock's outrageous terms. Another mark of his rashness is how willing he is to risk all he has on the voyages of four ships.

In contrast to this dark tale of hatred and prejudice is the love story of Portia and Bassanio. Like Antonio, Portia is bound by the law – in her case, the terms of her father's will. She is beautiful, and highly intelligent. The Prince of Morocco and the Prince of Aragon are not worthy of her. They choose the gold and silver caskets because they cannot see beyond outward appearances. It is the impoverished Bassanio who makes the right choice, and allows true love to win through.

Without Antonio's help, Portia and Bassanio would never have married, and that is why Portia decides to disguise herself as a lawyer, and travel to Venice to defend Antonio in court.

Shakespeare and the Globe Theatre

Some of Shakespeare's most famous plays were first performed at the Globe Theatre, which was built on the South Bank of the River Thames in 1599.

Going to the Globe was a different experience from going to the theatre today. The building was roughly circular in shape, but with flat sides: a little like a doughnut crossed with a fifty-pence piece. Because the Globe was an open-air theatre, plays were only put on during daylight hours in spring and summer. People paid a penny to stand in the central space and watch a play, and this part of the audience became known as 'the groundlings' because they stood on the ground. A place in the tiers of seating beneath the thatched roof, where there was a slightly better view and less chance of being rained on, cost extra.

The Elizabethans did not bath very often and the audiences at the Globe were smelly. Fine ladies and gentlemen in the more expensive seats sniffed perfume and bags of sweetly scented herbs to cover the stink rising from the groundlings.

There were no actresses on the stage; all the female characters in Shakespeare's plays would have been acted by boys, wearing wigs and make-up. Audiences were not well behaved. People clapped and cheered when their favourite actors came on stage; bad actors were jeered at and sometimes pelted with whatever came to hand.

Most Londoners worked hard to make a living and in their precious free time they liked to be entertained. Shakespeare understood the magic of the theatre so well that today, almost four hundred years after his death, his plays still cast a spell over the thousands of people that go to see them.

Orchard Classics
Shakespeare Stories

RETOLD BY ANDREW MATTHEWS
ILLUSTRATED BY TONY ROSS

Orchard Books are available from all good bookshops.